MY PURPOSE &

MY PURPOSE & PASSION
DEVOTIONAL

A 6-Chapter Journey for Women of Faith to Live with Purpose, Passion, and Reflection Every Day

LISA S. NORWOOD

MY PURPOSE & PASSION DEVOTIONAL

Copyright © 2025 by Lisa Norwood

All rights reserved. No part of this publication may be reproduced, distributed, or transmitted in any form or by any means, including photocopying, recording, or other electronic or mechanical methods, without the prior written permission of the author, except in the case of brief quotations used in reviews or articles.

Scripture quotations are taken from the Holy Bible, New International Version (NIV), unless otherwise noted.

For permissions or inquiries, contact:

iLead Education Services LLC Tempe, Arizona

www.ileadeducationservices.com

CONTENTS

Introduction IV

Purpose 1

Passion 14

Daily Intentions 30

Three Good Things 44

Positive Affirmations 56

Reflections 69

The Journey Continues 85

About The Author 88

INTRODUCTION

Welcome to *My Purpose and Passion Devotional.*

This devotional is a companion to *My Purpose and Passion Journal,* a space created to help you pause, reflect, and reconnect with who God designed you to be. I hope that as you read these chapters, you will begin to see that purpose is not something you chase. It is something you uncover as you walk faithfully with God.

Each chapter includes stories from my own life, moments filled with valleys, victories, and lessons learned along the way. You will also find "Pause and Reflect" moments that invite you to write, pray, and listen to God's whisper in your own journey.

Whether you are in a season of discovery, rediscovery, or deep transformation, I want you to remember this truth. You were created on purpose and for purpose. God has already placed everything you need within you. This devotional simply helps you see it more clearly. *Let us begin.*

"Purpose is not discovered in a moment. It unfolds as you walk with God, one whispered yes at a time."

1

PURPOSE

****

What does it mean to have purpose? How do you know what your purpose is? How do you know when your purpose aligns with what God would have you do? And what do you do when what you believe is your purpose is not what God intended? These questions matter because discovering your purpose shapes the way you live, lead, love, and show up in this world.

Sometimes God interrupts our plans not to frustrate us but to remind us that He sees far beyond what we can see. When that interruption comes, it is an invitation to pause, seek His direction, and trust that He is leading you toward a purpose designed specifically for who He created you to be.

In *Genesis 12–21,* Abram and Sarai understood this tension well. They knew what it felt like to hold onto a plan that seemed reasonable and familiar, yet completely different from the path God was calling them to walk. When God told Abram to leave everything he knew, there was no blueprint and no timeline. All he had was a promise and a choice. Trust God or trust his own understanding.

For years, Abram and Sarai carried the weight of a purpose they could not fully see. God promised them a child, yet their circumstances suggested the opposite. They questioned, they wrestled, they waited, and at times they tried to fix things on their own. Even in their doubt, God never abandoned the purpose He spoke over their lives.

Their story reminds us that purpose is rarely about what makes sense in the moment. Purpose is following God when the road does not look like the promise. It is trusting Him when the timing feels off or the path feels unclear. God's purpose will always stretch us beyond what we think we can handle.

There will be seasons when God redirects us, not to punish us but to position us. When what we thought was our purpose no longer aligns with His will, He is preparing us for something greater. Purpose unfolds over time, and every step of faith draws us closer to the life He designed for us.

Pause and Reflect

1. Think about a time when your plans did not match God's plans. How did you respond?

   _____

   _____

   _____

2. Where might God be redirecting you right now? Where is He inviting you to trust Him more than your own understanding?

   _____

   _____

   _____

Have you ever seen someone wake up each day with no real intentions, simply moving through the hours without direction? I often wonder if they know their purpose or if they even believe they have one. Maybe you have felt that way yourself at some point.

For as long as I can remember, my purpose felt rooted in one decision. I wanted to live differently from my parents. Not because I did not love them, but because somewhere along the way both of them lost their sense of purpose. My mom was brilliant, a gifted medical professional, until drinking consumed her life. My dad was intelligent and skilled, working as an inspector for Lockheed, until addiction pulled him away from his potential.

I knew I did not want to live without purpose. I wanted to make intentional choices that mattered. That desire shaped so much of who I became.

For many years, I believed my purpose was to be a mother, work, and care for my home. When I married in 1991, I lived fully in that purpose. I was a wife, a mother, a homemaker, and I built a career in education. Then God moved us from California to Phoenix, and that transition began a major redirection. Nineteen years of marriage ended, and everything I thought I understood about my purpose was shaken.

I had to start over.

Around that same time, I joined social media for the first time. When the profile asked me to describe myself, I typed *Reinventing Lisa*. I had no idea how accurate that description would be for the journey ahead.

Walking in your God given purpose fuels the passion you need to move forward. You were created on purpose and for purpose. God was intentional with every detail of who you are. And even if your purpose is not clear yet, that does not mean it is absent. Once you discover it, you will walk in it confidently, grateful that God carved a path specifically for you.

Detours will come. They are not meant to destroy you. They are meant to develop you. Some detours will test your faith. Some will make you question everything. Some will bring tears. Others may even make you laugh at God's timing, just as Sarah did in *Genesis 18:12–15*.

Without those lessons, your purpose cannot be fulfilled.

When I began my master's program in educational leadership, one of our first assignments was a Journey Line. We drew a large L shaped chart and marked the hills and valleys of our lives. It was a powerful activity. As I mapped my journey, I noticed more valleys than peaks. When I shared it with the group, I teared up. I am rarely emotional, but speaking those valleys aloud brought back years of pain.

Yet God was faithful.

Every valley prepared me for a greater purpose. Every low moment held a lesson I needed. That day I realized something important. Every stage of life has purpose, and each stage leads to the next.

Just like Abram and Sarai, even when I was not obedient, God remained faithful. He never gave up on me. He had purpose for my life long before I understood it.

Joseph's story in *Genesis 37–50* takes this truth even deeper. God had a specific purpose for Joseph, and nothing could cancel it. Joseph was deeply loved by his father, which made his brothers jealous. Out of envy, they sold him into slavery. That was his first detour. Yet even in slavery, he used his God given gifts and rose in Potiphar's house, just as described in *Genesis 39:2–6.*

Here is the lesson. Do not become too comfortable where you are. If Joseph had his way, he would have stayed with his father forever. But God had a bigger plan, and that plan required pulling him away from his comfort.

Pause and Reflect

1. Think of a time when God removed you from your comfort zone. What did that season teach you?

   _____
   _____
   _____

2. What comforts might be holding you back from your next level of purpose?

   _____
   _____
   _____

3. How might obedience in discomfort open the door to your destiny?

_____

_____

_____

Then came another detour. Potiphar's wife desired Joseph. He resisted out of loyalty to God. She lied, and he was imprisoned as recorded in *Genesis 39:7–20*. Even in chains, Joseph remained faithful. He continued to serve. He did not complain, and he did not quit.

Life often works the same way. You are moving forward, everything seems fine, and then an unexpected obstacle appears out of nowhere.

I experienced this myself. After earning my master's in educational leadership, I believed a principal position was next. But God delayed that dream. It was not a long delay, but it felt like a setback. In that season, I felt like Abram, Sarai, and Joseph. God reminded me that delay is not denial. Delay is often preparation.

Purpose and timing come from God, and His timing rarely matches ours. Yet His timing always strengthens our faith.

Joseph's story teaches us something powerful. Your current place is not your permanent position. God uses every stop, even the painful ones, to build something stronger within you.

Pause and Reflect

1. How do you respond when your plans are interrupted?

   _____
   _____
   _____

2. In what area is God asking you to remain faithful right now?

   _____
   _____
   _____

3. How can you choose gratitude in the middle of your detour?

_____
_____
_____

Purpose requires surrender. You cannot fully walk in God's will while holding onto your own. Until you give Him your whole heart, your habits, your relationships, and your fears, your purpose will always feel delayed. God does not want partial devotion. He desires all of you.

So, ask yourself: What is keeping me from fully surrendering?

Life gets overwhelming. The kids act up. Your spouse frustrates you. Friends drift. The job drains you. Church folks can be difficult. But at some point, you have to make a decision. You have to choose to serve God anyway. You have to stop making excuses and lean into the path He is showing you.

Joseph did not let betrayal or imprisonment stop him. He knew who sustained him. Because he stayed faithful, God blessed him in every season. His purpose was bigger than betrayal and bigger than the prison walls that confined him.

Pause and Reflect

1. What might full surrender look like for you right now?

   _____
   _____
   _____

2. What are you still trying to control instead of releasing to God?

   _____
   _____
   _____

3. How could your obedience today accelerate your purpose tomorrow?

   _____
   _____
   _____

When I reflect on Abram, Sarai, and Joseph, I am reminded that everything will be alright, even when I cannot see the outcome. God redirected my purpose just as He redirected theirs. I served as a principal for ten years and expected to retire in that position. Abram and Sarai expected to remain childless. We all believed we understood the path before us.

Then God shifted everything. He removed me from principalship and placed me on a new road filled with fresh lessons, deeper faith, and fuller surrender.

Your purpose was written long before you were born. Every detour, every delay, and every disappointment is still part of God's plan. Trust the process. God is not finished with you.

Closing Prayer

Father, thank You for creating me on purpose and for purpose. Help me trust Your plan even when detours come. Teach me to surrender every part of my life to You and to walk boldly in what You have called me to do. Strengthen my faith so that I remain obedient in every season. Guide my steps, calm my heart, and remind me that Your timing is perfect. In Jesus' name, Amen.

Reflections of Chapter 1

2

PASSION

***

What is your passion? What is that one thing that drives you? What is the one thing that keeps you up at night in deep thought? Most people are passionate about something. They have that one subject they could talk about forever and a day.

But what about people who do not know what their passion is? What about those who struggle to find that one thing that moves them? Can passion be discovered or even taught? How do you find it? Where do you look? Is it hidden in a book, a sermon, a conversation, or a moment of stillness?

According to Webster's dictionary, passion is "a strong feeling of enthusiasm or excitement for or devotion to some activity, object, or concept." When I read that definition, two things immediately come to mind for me personally: education and God.

My passion for God started when I was a young girl. In spite of my unstable childhood, I was blessed to attend a private Christian school from third grade to tenth grade and a private Christian college during my freshman and sophomore years.

During this time, I memorized Bible verses, attended chapel services every week, gave presentations about Bible characters, and attended worship every Sunday and Bible study on Wednesday nights. And we certainly cannot forget the special programs.

When I was sixteen, I began teaching Sunday School to the preschool and kindergarten students. My co-teacher taught me so much about preparing lessons and engaging children.

Who knew that this would be my first introduction to my passion for education?

Once I graduated from college, I became more involved in various ministries at church. I transitioned from teaching the littles to teaching ladies' Bible class, speaking at women's programs, and coordinating ministries for women at several congregations.

I can honestly say that church is the place where my passion for teaching and my passion for God were planted, not realizing that these passions would expand into a full career in education.

Like the detours mentioned in Chapter One, my life took the long route to bring me back to education. God knew I needed the lessons along the way to help me become a better educator, one whose purpose and passion would remain connected for the long haul.

Before we go deeper, let me pause to say this. Passion is not always loud. It is not always obvious. It does not always arrive fully formed. Sometimes passion grows quietly over time. Sometimes you resist it at first. And sometimes God hides it in places you never thought to look, until the right season reveals it.

Have you ever been in a job interview where they ask, "What is your greatest strength and your greatest weakness?" I remember being asked that many times, and my answer was always the same. My passion for education. It has been both a strength and a weakness, a blessing and at times a burden.

Let me explain.

My education journey was not my intention. It was God's doing. *Philippians 2:13* says, *"For it is God who works in you to will and to act in order to fulfill His good purpose."* My placement in a third-grade classroom at McKinley School in 1996 was orchestrated by God. That single moment opened a world where my passion for education grew and where I began to understand my purpose.

Passion without purpose leads to burnout. Purpose without passion leads to boredom. But passion aligned with purpose is fulfillment.

Education became both my purpose and my passion.

During my first year of teaching, I formed close relationships with experienced teachers who taught me the best strategies. They were wise, witty, and full of grace. I soaked up everything I could.

One teacher, Mrs. Collins, became my mentor, friend, and later sorority sister. She was deeply passionate about education and policy. She understood the laws that governed schools and fiercely advocated for both students and teachers. She encouraged me to attend my first education conference, and her advocacy showed me what true passion looked like in action.

As my passion grew, something interesting happened. It shifted.

My passion began with teaching students. Then it grew into teaching women. Then it expanded into coaching teachers. Coaching eventually led me into principalship, where I taught, coached, and led both adults and children.

The amazing part is that I did not fully recognize what God was doing. I only knew that my interest in education grew deeper, my purpose grew stronger, and my heart wanted to impact more people.

Fast forward to today. My passion for education remains both my strength and my weakness. It is my strength because I always fight for what is best for students, even if it means challenging the status quo. It is also my weakness for the very same reason.

As a principal, I made sure my staff understood one core value. Every decision must be made in the best interest of students, no exceptions. At the same time, my passion could make me overly determined. I made bold decisions alone, sometimes too quickly. I spoke up when others stayed silent. Some called it advocacy. Others called it being outspoken. I call it passion.

Pause and Reflect

1. What are you passionate about?

   _____
   _____
   _____

2. What activities, causes, or conversations make you feel alive?

   _____
   _____
   _____

3. How do you know that God guides your passion?

_____
_____
_____

4. Is your passion connected to your purpose? Are you fulfilled by both? Why or why not?

_____
_____

Passion is powerful, but it must be connected to God's calling. Passion without God's direction can become destructive or self-focused. Passion surrendered to God becomes fuel for kingdom work.

Let us look at a biblical character who displayed passion in both negative and positive ways—Saul, who later became Paul.

In *Acts 7,* Saul appears as Stephen is being stoned. He approved of the killing and held the coats of those throwing the stones. In *Acts 8,* he continues persecuting Christians. In *Acts 9,* everything changes. On the road to Damascus, Saul is confronted by Jesus Himself.

God transformed Saul's passion from persecution to proclamation. The same zeal he once used to destroy the church became the fire that spread the gospel. *Acts 9:20* says, *"He began to preach about Jesus immediately."*

Saul's transformation into Paul marked the moment when his passion became aligned with God's purpose. The very energy he once used for evil, God redirected for good.

Pause and Reflect

1. How has God redirected your energy or passion in a new way?

_____

_____

_____

2. What past experiences might He be redeeming for His purpose?

_____

_____

_____

3. Are there passions in your life that need God's realignment?

_____

_____

_____

Paul's story teaches us that passion must be aligned with God's direction. When it is, passion becomes powerful.

Another example of God aligned passion is Nehemiah. When he learned that Jerusalem's walls were destroyed, his heart broke. He prayed, fasted, and sought God's favor to rebuild. You can read this in *Nehemiah 1*. His passion drove him to act, and the king granted him permission to rebuild, even providing the resources needed.

Despite constant opposition, Nehemiah pressed on. He prayed before every decision and through every hardship. He prayed before speaking to the king, during attacks, when workers were tired, and when the wall was complete. He prayed through it all.

His story shows us that passion requires prayer. Nehemiah's mission was not about personal glory. It was about God's will and the restoration of His people. With God's help, the wall was rebuilt in only fifty-two days.

My journey as a principal in three different schools and three different districts reminds me of Nehemiah's assignment.

The first school I inherited as principal had a long list of challenges, from low academics to unmotivated staff to minimal family engagement. Challenges that most first-year principals would run from or crumble under.

But God.

He guided me through turning that school around. In one year, we exited school improvement status with the state. We were recognized for high academic growth. It felt like watching walls go up, fast and steady, with God's favor covering every step.

Nehemiah rebuilt the wall in fifty-two days. We rebuilt a school in record time. Passion, grit, and purpose worked together.

Over the next five years, we fully transformed the school. And like Nehemiah, we faced opposition, endured moments of joy, and survived seasons of war. That time required constant prayer, meditation, and leadership rooted in Scripture. I studied the lives of Jesus, David, Nehemiah, Esther, and many other biblical leaders to guide my decisions.

I walked boldly as a principal because God did not just answer my prayer to become a leader. He shaped me into one.

Pause and Reflect

1. Do you pray about your passion? If so, how? If not, why not?

   _____
   _____
   _____

2. How can you invite God into the center of your passion?

   _____
   _____
   _____

3. Are you passionate about a cause? If not, what stirs your heart? If so, how is that passion reflected in your life today?

   _____
   _____
   _____

Passion is not only about what excites you. It is about what moves you to act for God's glory.

There are countless causes worth standing behind. Often, passion comes from personal experience, whether hardship, victory, or healing.

When I left principalship in 2023, I thought my passion for education had reached its end. I did not understand what God was doing. I did not understand His timing. In my mind, I was supposed to retire as a principal. But God sent a massive detour.

That detour transformed my passion for education and my passion for Him into something bigger. And now here I am, an entrepreneur. Who would have imagined that?

Entrepreneurship is one of those journeys where purpose and passion must walk together. It requires strength and resilience. The learning curve is steep, the calling is heavy, and the sacrifices are real. You must be intentional in every part of your life and passionate about what you bring to the world.

You cannot sell something you do not believe in. My passion for better educational outcomes is what drives me now, because my impact is no longer limited to one school. It has expanded across districts, states, and entire communities.

It reminds me of Abram before he became Abraham. God promised him one son, then promised him nations. Transformation always begins with a seed.

My prayer life has deepened. My study of Scripture has become richer. My dependence on God has grown stronger.

Your passion matters because it reveals what God placed in your heart to change. Let Him guide it. Let Him grow it. When passion meets prayer, miracles happen.

Closing Prayer

Father, thank You for placing passion deep within my heart. Thank You for the gifts, the nudges, the desires, and the callings that lead me closer to Your purpose for my life. Help me recognize the passions You have planted and surrender them to Your guidance. Redirect anything in me that is misaligned. Revive anything that has grown weary. Reveal anything that is waiting to come alive. Strengthen me to use my passion for Your glory, with courage, clarity, and confidence. In Jesus' name, Amen.

Reflections of Chapter 2

3

DAILY INTENTIONS

***

Intention is defined as an aim or plan, an idea that you choose to carry out. Setting intentions keeps you grounded and focused on what truly matters. It gives direction to your day and purpose to your actions.

God modeled intentionality from the very beginning. In *Genesis 1,* His creation unfolded through a clear plan. Each day began with purpose, *"Let there be..."* and each day He completed what He started. When we live with intention, we reflect the heart of our Creator.

Getting to a place of intentional living takes time and practice. It is easy to talk about it now because I am living it, but my life was not always this way.

In Chapter One, I shared about my divorce after nineteen years. That season marked the beginning of a time when I did not know if I was coming or going. I was not living. I was barely existing mentally, physically, and financially. My life felt completely out of control. I was embarrassed, lost, and lonely. My middle and youngest sons struggled right alongside me, and their behavior reflected the pain and instability they were feeling. My oldest son was away at college, so he did not see it directly, but it would show up differently in him years later.

During these three years, I suffered my first of several mini strokes. The stress of trying to manage everything by myself weighed heavily on me. Right before my stroke, my car was repossessed. I will never forget riding the bus to work with my son beside me on his way to school. The shame of that season was suffocating.

I eventually started therapy and joined a divorce support group to help stabilize my mind and emotions. Nothing about that time reflected intentional living. But I kept going. I stayed connected to my church family, even through the embarrassment. That consistent connection was one of the first intentional steps I took, even when I did not realize it.

I started to see the light again when I entered my master's program at Arizona State University. God intervened in a way I did not think was possible. My entire program was fully funded. That moment was the beginning of me choosing to live intentionally. I saw God working, and I knew I needed to honor Him by making better choices.

Being intentional is not about perfection. It is about focus. It is choosing what gets your time, your energy, and your attention, on purpose.

Yes, God had a master plan for the world, but even He did not create it all in one day. Each day had a specific focus and an intended outcome. We can learn from this divine order. Each day has its own purpose, and when we plan with intention, we move closer to what God has called us to do.

As a former teacher, I lived by lesson plans. I outlined what I intended to teach each week, each day, and sometimes each hour. The goal was clarity. What outcomes did I want to see? What would success look like for students? When we plan with God, He becomes our co-teacher in the classroom of life.

I also love the story of Ruth as an example of intentional living. You can read her story in *Ruth 1–4*. Ruth married into a good family, but life shifted dramatically when her husband died, along with her father-in-law and brother-in-law. Three widows were suddenly left to figure out how to move forward. Naomi urged her daughters-in-law to return to their families, but Ruth refused. Her words still echo with power, *"Your people will be my people, and your God will be my God."* Ruth understood the assignment.

Naomi made intentional choices to position them near her late husband's relatives, and Ruth followed her instructions step by step. Her diligence and obedience placed her directly in the path of Boaz, the man who would eventually become her husband. Their lineage would lead to the birth of Jesus. Sometimes loss becomes the soil where God's goodness begins to grow.

Winston Churchill once said, "He who fails to plan is planning to fail." Without daily intention, our time slips quietly through our fingers.

Ephesians 5:15–16 tells us, *"Be careful how you live, not as unwise but as wise, making the most of every opportunity, because the days are evil."*

Pause and Reflect

1. What does an intentional day look like for you?

   _____
   _____
   _____

2. Where in your life are you losing valuable time and focus?

   _____
   _____
   _____

3. How can you invite God to help you plan your days more purposefully?

   _____
   _____
   _____

Before we continue, we need to talk about what intentional living is not.

Intentional living is not:

- doing everything

- saying yes to everyone

- operating from perfectionism

- moving without praying

- grinding until you are exhausted

- reacting instead of planning

Being intentional means doing the right things. How do you know what the right things are? That takes us back to Chapters One and Two. What is your purpose? What is your passion? Are they aligned with God's plan for your life?

And if they are, what intentional actions do you need to take each day to fulfill that purpose and passion?

Purpose gives direction. Passion gives energy. Intentions turn both into movement.

Remember Nehemiah. He had a plan and a goal before he ever approached the king. And before he talked to the king, he talked to God. His planning matched his obedience.

When was the last time you talked to God about your plan? Do you talk to Him about your daily intentions?

Start small. Pray first. Then write three to five intentions for your day, simple steps that keep you aligned with your purpose.

Every small act of obedience matters. Obedience begins with prayer and alignment. *Proverbs 21:5* reminds us, *"The plans of the diligent lead surely to abundance."*

In my new role as a Founder and CEO, I plan each week just as I did as a teacher and principal. I pray over my plans and about my plans. I pray for God to lead me to the right clients, not perfect ones. I want every appointment, every meeting, and every project to align with the work God has called me to do.

This entrepreneurial journey looks different from what I am used to, but the structure is the same.

Let me share what that shift looked like for me.

As a principal, I went to the same place every day, worked with the same people, and followed a familiar schedule.

Now, as an entrepreneur, my work varies. I work from home, visit multiple campuses, and support teachers and leaders with different needs depending on the contract.

New routines had to be created. My expectations had to shift. My focus had to broaden. And because I do not see school leaders and teachers every day, I have to be intentional about the time we do have together. When I leave, I hope that they carry out the strategies we planned and stay committed long after I am gone.

Prayer. Planning. Intentions.

Pause and Reflect

1. What three intentions could you set for tomorrow morning?

   _____
   _____
   _____

2. How do your current routines align with your bigger purpose?

   _____
   _____
   _____

3. What distractions do you need to surrender to God to reclaim your focus?

   _____
   _____
   _____

If you are wondering where to start, here is a simple way to set daily intentions with God:

1. **Start with prayer**.

    - *This connects you to God's voice and guidance.*

2. **Read the Bible daily.**

    - *Scripture reminds you of who God is and how He moves.*

3. **Journal your reflections.**

    - *Writing helps you merge what you read with where you are and where God is leading you.*

4. **Choose one intention that aligns with your purpose.**

    - *Even one focused step can shift everything.*

5. **Reflect at night.**

    - *Acknowledge where you saw God working and where you need His help tomorrow.*

Colossians 3:23 says, *"Whatever you do, work heartily, as for the Lord and not for men."*

Intentional living is less about perfection and more about partnership with God. When your intentions align with His purpose, even the smallest actions carry eternal impact.

Society tells us intentional living is about doing more. But intentionality is about doing what matters. It is about being purposeful, efficient, and present. It is about using your time wisely and investing in the people and tasks that support your God given purpose.

It is also important to understand the difference between intentional living and simple goal setting.

Intentional living aligns your daily actions with your purpose and passion. It is active. It is deliberate. It is doing.

Goal setting is writing down the things you want to accomplish. It is thoughtful, but not active. It is planned.

Both are useful, but intentional living brings movement.

Pause and Reflect

1. How can you make your work, paid or unpaid, an act of worship this week?

   _____
   _____
   _____

2. When was the last time you paused to ask God what He wanted you to do today?

   _____
   _____
   _____

3. How might your day look different if you started it with gratitude and intentional prayer?

   _____
   _____
   _____

God was intentional about creating the world and about creating you. I want my life to reflect that same intentionality, and I encourage you to do the same. Do the important things. Block out the distractions.

As you practice setting daily intentions, you will begin to see how much more you accomplish and how much more peace fills your days. Remember, intentional living is not about getting things done. It is about walking in alignment with God's will, one day at a time.

CLOSING PRAYER

God, help me live each day with purpose and intention. Guide my thoughts, my plans, and my actions so they reflect Your will. Teach me to use my time wisely and to focus on what truly matters. Let every moment of my day bring honor to You. Amen.

Reflections of Chapter 3

4

THREE GOOD THINGS

***

In a world filled with negativity, division, and constant noise, we must be intentional about noticing the good. Gratitude is not accidental. It is a discipline. A choice. A spiritual practice that aligns our hearts with the heart of God.

God modeled this from the very beginning.

In *Genesis 1,* after every act of creation, He paused, looked at what He made, and reflected:

"God saw that it was good." - (Genesis 1:4, 10, 12, 18, 21, 25)

If the Creator of the universe took time to acknowledge the good, how much more should we?

Recognizing the good is not ignoring what is hard. It is choosing gratitude in the midst of it. It is shifting your focus from what drains you to what strengthens you. It is choosing, day by day, to see God's fingerprints.

But for me, this lesson did not come easily.

As a principal, I could walk into a classroom and spot five things wrong within thirty seconds, and my face showed it. Teachers dreaded my presence because I carried a spirit of correction instead of encouragement. One day my leadership team challenged me:

"Every time you visit a classroom, find three good things."

I did not like it.

And honestly, it was hard.

My mind was trained to look for gaps, mistakes, and things that needed to be fixed. I was a problem solver by nature, so good was not at the top of my radar. But as I practiced, everything changed. My attitude, my awareness, my relationships, and eventually the culture of my school.

Goodness had always been present. I just was not slowing down long enough to see it. Gratitude softens what correction alone can never heal.

Pause and Reflect

1. When was the last time you intentionally stopped to notice something good in your day?

   _____

   _____

   _____

2. How might focusing on the good shift the atmosphere in your home, workplace, or relationships?

   _____

   _____

   _____

3. What does it say about God that He took time to call His creation good?

   _____

   _____

   _____

I wish I could say gratitude became my daily rhythm after that leadership shift. But life had more lessons to teach me.

During COVID, I suffered another mini stroke. This was my fourth one, and it came dangerously close to ending my life. My blood pressure was at an all-time high. I was admitted to the ICU for three days, waiting for answers.

The tests showed nothing. Nothing.

Then the neurologist came in and said something that changed everything:

"Your body does not know how to respond to stress. Your automatic response is stroke mode."

Her prescription was for a therapist who specialized in stress, something I did not even know existed. But God did. He knew exactly who and what I needed.

At my first session, the therapist told me,

"You have a lot of negative energy stored inside. We are going to work on releasing it."

Every week she had me list positive things, things I had ignored for years. She prescribed a gratitude journal and told me to start with one thing I was thankful for each day. Just one.

It was harder than it sounds.

With time, my sessions moved from weekly to monthly. But when God removed me from the principalship, they went back to biweekly. My therapist was doing everything she could to prevent a fifth mini stroke. When your life is shaken, good things do not come naturally. But step by step, week by week, my mindset began to shift.

Philippians 4:8 tells us:

"Whatever is true, whatever is noble, whatever is admirable, think about such things."

God calls us to elevate our focus. To discipline our minds. To choose what is worthy, not what is worrisome.

Science now confirms what Scripture has taught all along. Gratitude rewires the brain. It reduces stress, strengthens emotional resilience, and shifts your inner atmosphere.

As I embraced the practice, everything changed.

I began posting a daily gratitude list online, 365 Days of Thankfulness, every single day. Then I challenged myself to complete a second year. Eventually, I began journaling privately in my own *Grateful. Thankful. Blessed.* journal.

Now I am in year four of daily gratitude. The shift has been life giving. Healing. Transformative.

Do I still have moments? Absolutely. But negativity no longer consumes me. And that alone is a miracle I thank God for.

Pause and Reflect

1. Who in your life could benefit from you acknowledging something good about them this week?

　

2. How can you apply Philippians 4:8 to a current challenge?

　

3. What happens to your mindset when you speak gratitude instead of criticism?

Luke 6:45 says,

"A good man brings good things out of the good stored up in his heart."

Whatever you store internally is what will overflow when life squeezes you. If you store frustration, bitterness, or negativity, that is what spills out. But if you store gratitude, truth, joy, peace, and God's Word, your life produces something different.

People often say you cannot pour from an empty cup. I agree. But I will add this:

You cannot pour from a cup filled with toxic thoughts either.

For years, I allowed my trauma to shape my thinking. I was a Negative Nelly, and honestly, even I did not want to be around myself. But thank God for grace. Thank God for therapists. Thank God for a renewed mind.

Gratitude did not change my circumstances. It changed me.

Pause and Reflect

1. What are you storing in your heart, gratefulness or grumbling?

   _____
   _____
   _____

2. How can you model positivity in your workplace or home?

   _____
   _____
   _____

3. What are three good things in your life right now?

   _____
   _____
   _____

The Bible gives us powerful examples of people who chose goodness even in hard circumstances. Joseph's story reminds us that gratitude and faith are choices, not conditions. Despite betrayal, slavery, imprisonment, and being forgotten, he maintained integrity and trust in God. He even saved the very people who hurt him.

Barnabas, whose name means *son of encouragement,* saw potential where others saw problems. He uplifted the apostles, supported the poor, and believed in Paul when others doubted him. He carried goodness wherever he went.

May we all grow to be more like Joseph and Barnabas, people who choose the good even when life is difficult.

Try incorporating *Three Good Things* into your daily routine. Write down three good things each day. Speak them out loud. Share them with someone close to you. Send one encouraging text a day. Thank God for one thing you overlooked. Celebrate one small win every day. These small moments build spiritual muscle memory. They teach your heart to expect God.

They help you recognize blessings you once overlooked.

James 1:17 reminds us: *"Every good and perfect gift is from above."*

God saw that it was good. Can you see it too?

Closing Prayer

Heavenly Father, open my eyes to see the good around me. Even when life feels heavy or uncertain, remind me of Your faithfulness. Fill my heart with gratitude and my mouth with praise. Teach me to recognize Your blessings, celebrate what is good, and carry a spirit of encouragement wherever I go. Amen.

Reflections of Chapter 4

5

POSITIVE AFFIRMATIONS

Positive affirmations are declarations of truth about who we are and who we are becoming in God. God gave the first example when He said to Moses, *"I AM WHO I AM" (Exodus 3:14)*. When we speak affirmations rooted in Scripture, we are not creating a new identity. We agree with the one God already gave us.

Affirmations are not empty positivity. They are in spiritual agreement. When we declare God's Word over our lives, we shift our mindset from insecurity to identity. We stop rehearsing what the world said about us and start remembering what Heaven has already spoken. This is where transformation begins.

The truth is, many of us struggle to see ourselves the way God does. For years, I found it hard to speak well of myself. My belief about who I was had been shaped by childhood trauma. I rarely heard positive things spoken about me.

In fact, I was often told by family members that I would not amount to anything. I internalized those negative messages and carried them into adulthood.

It was strange. I desperately wanted to be celebrated, yet I had no idea how to receive celebration. I still struggle with being celebrated at times, but it is nothing like before.

Healing softens what once felt heavy.

So, the question becomes: If God created me in His image and called me good, who was I to say otherwise? That is something I am still working on today.

Genesis 1:27 reminds us, *"So God created mankind in His own image."*

Learning to shift my thinking according to God's Word did not happen overnight. It took intentional work, prayer, and time. And strangely enough, much of my growth happened while I was serving as a leader.

Leadership is not just about helping others be better. It is about allowing God to make you better. One of the biggest lessons I learned was the importance of building capacity in others. That meant encouraging people, identifying their strengths, and helping them grow. In order to do that, I had to start seeing the good in people, and eventually the good in myself. As I grew my staff, I grew myself.

There was one teacher I will never forget. She was new, incredibly talented, and had such a natural gift, but she could not see it. After her first year, she quit teaching because she did not believe she was good enough.

Fast forward to my second year as a principal. I needed a second-grade teacher. Guess who I called? Yes, her. She hesitated, but she came. Every year, I encouraged her to consider a leadership role. Every year, she said no.

Then one day, years later, I received a text message. She had gone back to school, earned her master's degree in curriculum and instruction, and was now working as an instructional coach. She thanked me for believing in her when she did not believe in herself.

That is the power of speaking life into others.

Biblically, this makes sense. Paul encouraged Timothy in the same way. In *2 Timothy 1:6-8,* Paul urges Timothy to use the gift God gave him. He reminds him that the Spirit gives us power, love, and self-control. Paul's words became the affirmation Timothy needed to step into his calling.

In schools, we had a saying: "Ask three before me." Students asked three classmates before coming to the teacher. Yes, it freed the teacher, but more importantly, it built confidence in the classmates. As they helped others, they strengthened what they knew.

Is that not how God works? As we speak truth into others, that truth takes root in us as well.

It takes work to shift how you see yourself in God. It will not happen overnight. But if you stay with it, transformation will come. As I began confronting old labels, God taught me to pay attention to the words I spoke over myself.

Pause and Reflect

1. How do you usually speak about yourself when no one is listening?

   _____
   _____
   _____

2. Which negative labels or lies have you believed that God never said about you?

   _____
   _____
   _____

3. How might your confidence change if you began each morning affirming what God says about you?

   _____
   _____
   _____

Affirmations become powerful when combined with faith and repetition. Write them down, say them aloud, and repeat them often. We truly do have to retrain our brains. Even science agrees with Scripture. Research on neuroplasticity shows that repeating positive, truth-based statements can rewire the brain. Negative thinking creates negative pathways. Truth creates new ones.

When God tells us to renew our minds *(Romans 12:2),* He is giving us a blueprint for transformation.

Do you remember the movie *The Help?* Aibileen taught Mae the phrase, "You is kind, you is smart, you is important." Just imagine if every child grew up hearing this daily. Our world would look different.

Words shape identity. They plant seeds, good or bad. And the words we speak over ourselves often shape the way we speak to others.

The Bible says, *"Do unto others as you would have them do unto you" (Matthew 7:12).*

Luke 6:31 puts it simply: *"Treat people like you want to be treated."*

We taught this every day in school. Students did not like being mistreated, yet some had no hesitation in mistreating others. Is that not our world today? We excuse mistreating others while demanding kindness for ourselves.

True biblical love calls us to something greater.

Matthew 22:37–39 teaches us to love God with all our heart, soul, and mind, and to love our neighbor as we love ourselves. You cannot love others well if you do not treat yourself well. And you cannot treat yourself well if you do not believe what God says about you.

A Few Affirmations I Practice Daily

- *I am smart.*

- *I am beautiful.*

- *I am kind.*

- *I am a leader.*

- *I am chosen by God to do great things.*

- *I am a daughter of the King.*

- *I am becoming who God created me to be.*

- *I am worthy of good things.*

- *I am walking in purpose on purpose.*

I need to see my affirmations. I write them on sticky notes in my office and on my bathroom mirror.

When my husband moved in after we married, he saw all the sticky notes on the mirror. He did not say anything at first. His expression said enough. I explained why they were there. He smiled and nodded. He understood.

Faith comes by hearing *(Romans 10:17)*. When you speak God's truth, your ears hear it and your heart begins to believe it.

Pause and Reflect

1. What truth do you need to speak over your life this week?

   _____
   _____
   _____

2. How could your affirmations serve as reminders of God's promises?

   _____
   _____
   _____

3. What is one "I AM" statement you could post somewhere visible as your daily declaration?

   _____
   _____
   _____

Affirmations Based on God's Word

- *I am created with God's hand. Isaiah 64:8*

- *I am royalty. 1 Peter 2:9*

- *I am fearfully and wonderfully made. Psalm 139:14*

- *I am powerful. 2 Timothy 1:7*

- *I am made in God's image. Genesis 1:27*

- *I am strong, courageous, and victorious. Exodus 14:14*

- *I am not alone. Isaiah 54:10*

We have to remind ourselves daily that we are enough. Satan wants us to believe we are not strong, not worthy, not loved. He uses small lies to chip away at our identity. That is why I keep my affirmations visible. My spirit needs the reminders.

How to Use Affirmations Daily

- Choose three to five Scriptures or truths.

- Speak them out loud every morning.

- Write them where you can see them daily.

- Pray them.

- Replace negative thoughts with truth immediately.

- Share them with someone else to reinforce them.

Pause and Reflect

1. What do you think God sees when He looks at you?

   _____
   _____
   _____

2. What is one area where you need to start believing you are enough?

   _____
   _____
   _____

3. How can you use affirmations not only for yourself but to uplift someone else this week?

_____

_____

_____

Your mindset will shift, and you will begin walking in purpose on purpose.

Closing Prayer

Lord, thank You for creating me in Your image. Teach me to see myself as You see me, worthy, loved, and chosen. Silence every negative voice and fill me with confidence in who You say I am. Let my words reflect Your truth daily. In Jesus' name, Amen.

Reflections of Chapter 5

6

REFLECTIONS

***

Reflection is where everything comes together. Purpose, passion, intentions, three good things, and affirmations all grow deeper when we pause long enough to notice what God is doing in us. Reflection is how we see His fingerprints in places we once overlooked. It is how we honor the journey that brought us here.

According to Merriam Webster, reflection is "a thought, idea, or opinion formed, or a remark made, as a result of meditation."

When I think about reflection, I think about alignment and spiritual awareness. I think about how, as a Christian, I am in constant reflection of my thoughts and my actions. I am repeatedly thinking about how I show up in different places.

If Heaven is our goal, daily reflection should be our way of life. Reading and meditating on God's Word. Understanding

His purpose for our lives. Using the passion He has placed in us to do great things that glorify Him.

Living intentionally each day, making the most of our time. Noticing the good things happening daily and affirming who we are in Christ.

Regular reflection improves our lives. It does not allow us to stay stuck. It does not allow us to keep making excuses.

And healthy reflection does not invite us into overthinking or spiraling. If you find yourself in either of those places, it may be time to step back and let God help you undo what got you there.

I remember during one of my many interviews after I left the principalship, I was asked a question I had never heard before: "What irritates you?" Me being me, I answered as authentically as I could. I said that people who do not show any forward progress irritate me. I do not understand how people do not have goals in life, how people make excuses for everything under the sun, and quite frankly, how people lack ambition.

What does this have to do with reflection? A reflective person is not stagnant. A reflective person is constantly thinking about how to be better and do better.

A reflective person looks at herself in the mirror.

"As in water the face reflects the face, so a man's heart reveals the man." (Proverbs 27:19)

Water reflects what is in front of it. A mirror shows what stands before it. Writing reveals what is within it.

Reflection allows us to pause, look back, and see who we are becoming. It is how God helps us realign our hearts with His.

Reflection is not always pretty. Sometimes it is painful.

When we reflect on our mistakes, guilt can rise to the surface. But even guilt can serve a holy purpose. It can lead us back to grace.

Take Judas, for example. He walked with Jesus, yet betrayed Him. His guilt consumed him *(Matthew 27:3–5)*.

Guilt condemns, but conviction corrects. When God convicts us, it is not to shame us. It is to draw us closer.

Pause and Reflect

1. When was the last time you felt convicted about something? How did you respond?

   _____
   _____
   _____

2. What is the difference between feeling guilty and allowing God to correct you?

   _____
   _____
   _____

3. How could reflection through repentance bring healing to your heart?

   _____
   _____
   _____

David gives us a picture of reflection that leads to redemption. In *2 Samuel 11–12,* after he committed adultery with Bathsheba and had her husband killed, David wrote *Psalm 51,* a prayer of repentance. His reflection became his restoration.

Writing your reflections, like David, allows you to express emotions, release burdens, and record growth. Reflection through writing becomes an act of worship.

I have never killed anyone or had anyone killed like David. But I have sinned in such a way that I was full of guilt.

Some sins are just between you and God. We often refer to those as "skeletons in your closet." We all have them.

The question becomes: Has the guilt of those skeletons led you to repent and reflect?

I can only speak for Lisa. My sin came from my own selfish desires, creating a narrative I wanted and going to great lengths to make it happen.

Afterwards, it did not feel as good as it sounded while I was conjuring it in my mind. The Spirit was working on me because I knew better. How could I stoop so low? How could I subject myself to such degradation? The guilt began to settle in, but even that took time. I carried that sin and guilt for about four years. Deep down, I knew it was time to take it to God in all my shame.

When I became a principal in 2013, I realized how far God had brought me and how He had blessed me and answered so many prayers. It was then I knew I could not keep going without asking God to forgive me for what I had done so many years earlier.

I cried. I journaled. I cried again. I was sick to my stomach. I knew that if I did not repent and ask God to forgive me, He might snatch my blessing away, and I did not want that at all.

So, I repented and asked for forgiveness.

But me being stubborn and prideful, it took another year before I asked the person, I had sinned against to forgive me. Five years of guilt. Five years of shame.

Like David, I journaled my sin. I journaled my repentance, and I journaled my prayer asking God to forgive me. And because I did not want anyone ever to find out about my sin, I burned the journal afterwards.

Pause and Reflect

1. What lesson has God been teaching you lately that is worth writing down?

   _____
   _____
   _____

2. How could journaling become a consistent part of your spiritual growth?

   _____
   _____

3. What is one area where you need to be honest with God today?

   _____
   _____
   _____

Reflection is not only for correction. It is also for celebration. God reflected on His creation and *saw that it was good (Genesis 1:31).*

David said in *Psalm 143:5,* *"I remember the days of long ago; I meditate on all Your works and consider what Your hands have done."*

Reflection and remembrance go hand in hand. When we reflect with gratitude, we magnify God's goodness and strengthen our faith.

When I think about reflection as celebration, I think about my life overall. I think about how far I have come. I think about how God has had His hand on my life.

In August 2024, I attended the Texas Women's Empowerment Conference in Dallas, Texas. It was one of the most impactful conferences I had attended in a long time. The speakers were powerful, speaking life into each woman in attendance.

During the conference, I purchased a book called *Surrender* by Tiffany Malone. I highly recommend this book. I did not start reading it until November 2024. When I tell you that book snatched my soul and got me all the way together!

There is a part of the book where she asks you to write out your life story, but from the lens of God working in your life and not from the victim mentality.

So, remember how, in the previous chapters, I spoke about my childhood traumas? Now I had to confront those traumas with positivity. I had to look at how God purposefully executed every situation to get me to where I am today.

This was a deep reflection into who Lisa Norwood really is and was. At the end of it all, I celebrated my life. I celebrated that even though I grew up without my parents, I had relatives who stepped in and raised me.

I celebrated that even though I was an only child, God surrounded me with women who became like sisters. I celebrated that my granny instilled a love for God in me that I carry to this day.

I reflected and celebrated every aspect of my life, and like God, I saw that it was for my good.

In August 2025, I attended TWEC again and was fortunate to be in a class with Tiffany Malone herself. God saw fit for me to be in her presence so I could thank her from the bottom of my heart for writing her book. I shared the transformation that occurred in me after reading it.

Pause and Reflect

1. What has God done in your life recently that deserves a moment of gratitude?

   _____
   _____
   _____

2. When was the last time you celebrated your own progress instead of downplaying it?

   _____
   _____
   _____

3. Who could you thank today for being part of your journey?

   _____

   _____

   _____

Jesus modeled reflection with His disciples in *John 13–16,* reflecting on His mission and God's promises. Reflection does not always have to happen in isolation. Sometimes it is best shared with those you trust.

Reflection with others makes me think about my leadership teams as a principal. In all three schools, I was blessed to have educators on my team that I could fully trust and who trusted me.

During the summers, we would reflect on the previous year. We looked at academic data, attendance data, behavior data, and any other data we had access to. The reflections allowed us to celebrate small wins and big wins. They helped us create action plans for what we wanted to do differently. We used that time to build connections as we planned for the next school year.

Reflection should become a rhythm, not a rare event. Try setting aside time each week to pause, pray, and write about what is on your heart. Invite others to reflect with you.

Reflection is more than looking back. It is looking deeper. When you see God's hand in your story, you begin to see that every chapter, every detour, and every delay had purpose all along.

This deep reflection happened to me in the space between leaving the principalship and becoming an entrepreneur. I spent a lot of time alone, just me and God. I studied more than I had in a long time. I read the stories of Joseph and Job numerous times. I needed to see how God worked in their lives after such horrible things happened to them.

Reading those stories gave me hope, renewed purpose, and a new outlook on my life. I was able to embrace the change taking place. Little by little, I could see God working. He gave me glimmers of hope that everything was going to be all right.

Then He really showed up for me.

In April 2023, I was supposed to have cochlear implant surgery, but there was a mix up with my school insurance. I was devastated because I had been waiting quite a while for approval.

Fast forward to July 2023. I was now using the insurance under my husband's plan. My cochlear implant surgery was rescheduled for September 2023. His insurance covered ninety nine percent of the surgery. Praise the Lord!

How is this connected to reflection? It was not until after my surgery that I saw the hand of God working miraculously on my behalf. In the weeks following my surgery, I was completely deaf in my left ear and had very little interaction with others. This became my time with God, reflecting on how the surgery even happened, how just six months earlier I had been denied due to a mix up, and how the surgery was now almost fully covered under my husband's insurance.

Reflecting on how God's redirection in my career was a setup for the rest of my life.

Reflection gives me clarity. Reflection gives me peace.

Reflection helps us honor where we have been so we can walk boldly into where God is taking us. When we slow down long enough to see His hand in our story, we realize we were never alone, not for a moment. Every chapter, every tear, every breakthrough, every delay was shaping us into who we are today.

Reflection turns our lives into testimonies, and testimonies into praise.

Pause and Reflect

1. What is God teaching you in this current season of your life?

   _____

   _____

   _____

2. How has your story, and the way you see it, changed over the years?

   _____

   _____

   _____

3. Where do you see God's grace woven into your journey right now?

_____

_____

_____

Closing Prayer

Gracious God, thank You for the gift of reflection. Help me to pause, listen, and learn from every season of my life. When I look back, let me see Your hand in every detail. Continue to shape my heart and renew my spirit as I walk forward in faith. Amen.

Reflections of Chapter 6

MY PURPOSE & PASSION DEVOTIONAL

THE JOURNEY CONTINUES

***

You've reached the end of these pages, but you haven't reached the end of your journey. In fact, this is the beginning of a new one, shaped by clarity, intention, faith, and purpose.

Over these six chapters, you've explored who you are, why you're here, and how God is shaping you day by day. You've looked at your purpose with fresh eyes. You've reclaimed your passion. You've set intentions that align with God's will. You've noticed good things you once overlooked. You've affirmed your identity in Christ. And you've reflected on the path that brought you here.

And now... You are being invited to live it out.

Not perfectly. Not flawlessly.

Not fearlessly every day. But faithfully.

God never asked you to have it all figured out. He simply asked you to walk with Him, one prayer, one intention, one affirmation, one reflection at a time. Your story is still being written. Your growth is still unfolding. Your purpose is still calling.

And God is still guiding, still loving, still speaking, still restoring.

As you step forward, keep writing. Keep listening. Keep trusting. Keep reflecting. And when life gets loud or heavy or uncertain, return to these practices. They will anchor you. They will remind you who you are. They will point you back to the One who has been with you from the very beginning.

My prayer is that these pages have sparked something new in you, a renewed desire to know God, to love yourself, and to embrace the future He designed for you.

May your journey ahead be full of grace.

May your purpose shine brighter.

May your passion burn stronger.

May your intentions keep you focused.

May your reflections keep you grounded.

And may the God who began a good work in you continue carrying it to completion.

This isn't goodbye. This is *forward*.

Walk boldly, because you do not walk alone.

—*Lisa*

ABOUT THE AUTHOR

***

Lisa Norwood is a woman of faith, purpose, and perseverance. A 25-year educator turned leadership coach and consultant, she has devoted her life to helping others discover their God-given potential and lead with purpose and grace.

As the founder of *iLead Education Services*, Lisa has guided schools, leaders, and organizations through transformation, empowering them to build systems that last. But beyond her professional accomplishments, her greatest calling is inspiring people to believe that their past does not define their future.

Born from her own journey of healing and rediscovery, *My Purpose & Passion Devotional* invites readers to slow down, listen for God's voice, and walk boldly in the identity He designed for them. Lisa believes that purpose and passion are not found; they are revealed through faith, surrender, and daily obedience.

When she's not writing or coaching, Lisa enjoys walking near the water, worshiping God, traveling, listening to live music, and spending quiet moments with family and friends. She lives each day with gratitude for God's grace and a renewed sense of purpose.

Made in the USA
Coppell, TX
23 December 2025

65025042R00056